How to Attend a Conference
Like a Bootstrapped
Entrepreneur

Heather Diamani

Table of Contents

Introduction

Attending conferences can be expensive, but it doesn't have to be. The key is creating a budget and sticking to it, so you are able to attend the conferences that will help your career.

When I first started my business, I knew that attending conferences would be beneficial to my success, but I also thought as a startup it would be tough to scrap up some extra money to go.

I decided to research the best possible ways to attend a conference, while saving the most money I could. I found that it doesn't have to be expensive, and now I want to share these tips with you.

Whether you are a startup business, a blogger, or you have been in business for a long time, everyone can benefit from attending a conference. Plus, anybody could do with saving some money with their business travel.

Part One:
Pre-Conference Research

Section 1: The Benefits of Attending Conferences

Some people like to attend conferences, some do not, and others may be just neutral. Well, I happen to love attending conferences. I enjoy the atmosphere, learning, and meeting new people.

Attending conferences presents opportunities to meet and connect with new people, to learn, and to meet potential companies to work with or hire in the future.

Some benefits of attending conferences…

Help you learn to improve in an area
If you're still learning about topics in your industry, attending sessions will help expand your knowledge and arm you with tips and tricks from the experts.

Learn about key issues and how to resolve them

If there are legal issues with your industry that you're not aware of, it could put your business at risk. Therefore, it is essential to stay on top of the latest issues.

Networking value

Networking is valuable for meeting and connecting with like-minded people, and you never know who you'll meet and connect with. When business is discussed, sometimes people can offer up new ideas and change the way you approach a problem.

Learn new trends

If there is a new industry trend, being up to date will enhance your skills or help you learn something new.

Discover current tools and technologies

New tools are popping up often, and knowing which tool to use can help boost your business.

Promote yourself, your brand, and your business

Word of mouth and social media are ways to promote yourself, brand or business, but showing up and promoting your business personally is essential, too. Not everyone will know about you and your business just from the Internet alone, so the more ways to promote yourself, the better.

Regain your focus

Sometimes people procrastinate or fall off track and start slacking, but attending conferences can help you regain focus.

Get motivated and renew your excitement for your business

The excitement for a new business is usually high at first, but you want and need it to last. The atmosphere at a conference alone is enough to regenerate excitement, but the sessions and networking really can amp you up, as well.

Meet experts and mentors

Meeting experts and mentors gives you a chance to ask them questions and attend a session if they're giving one. Sometimes just meeting someone who's an expert may inspire you to work harder to reach your goals.

Improve productivity

When attending sessions, watching how someone else works can make you want to improve your productivity, because you'll gain insight on how to do something better and work may become easier.

Increased creativity and new ideas for your business
Once you're in sessions learning, ideas start popping up like popcorn. Sometimes the ideas come so fast, and there are so many, that you may be worried to lose them (always jot them down). I can't tell you how many notebooks I've gone through when I first started attending conferences. I kept having "Ah-hah!" moments and thinking "Ooooh, I have the best idea!" Eventually I stopped writing, because my hand hurt and there was too much paper, so I switched to using Evernote or a Word document on my laptop.

Being around like-minded people can be inspirational and refreshing
If you work from home, it's nice to get out and mingle with like-minded people. Personally, a lot of my friends in my town aren't into the same business and tech stuff as me, so when I get the chance to go to a conference I get to meet up with new people and friends that live elsewhere but speak the same language as me. There's also a chance to meet some really inspiring people.

Gain insight and experience
When attending a conference, you can gain insight on how other companies run and you also gain professional experience from attending.

Identify opportunities
If you had already identified opportunities before the conference, you'll find more while being there and for the next conference, as well.

Section 2: Are You Ready to Attend a Conference?

How do you know you're ready and whether it is worth it to attend?

If you have never been to a conference, and you are just starting out in a new field, but have tons of questions and need guidance, then a conference can present many opportunities and solutions for you.

But not just any conference, of course. You will need to look into which one is right for you.

Some people procrastinate and say things like "One day I'll go" or "I just haven't had the time", but that's just an excuse. When is the time ever right?

No time is ever just right, because there's always something going on. The circumstances may change, but it's the mindset that needs to change as well. If you think you can't... you won't. If you think you can... you will.

Note: If you are looking to exhibit at a conference, but finances are tight, it is best to continue building your company and hold off on exhibiting until the next time around or the time after that.

Section 3: Choosing a Conference

There are plenty of conferences that happen each year, but how do you know which one is right for you?

Don't base it off of how much money it costs; instead, identify the right conference by answering these questions:

What is the conference about?

Check to see what topics are covered at the conference. If the conference is for SEO experts, and you're a beginner in affiliate marketing, then it'd best not to go to that one. If the conference offers various topics of your interest at different experience levels, then that conference would be a great choice.

Does it pertain to my business?

If the conference is for electronics, and your business does not sell electronics, why waste time going to a conference like that? The conference should benefit you, and your business, in multiple ways.

What will the sessions be like?

Are the sessions short, long, advanced, or all on one topic? Are there various topics being presented? Make sure there will be topics of your interest and make sure to know which pass to purchase so you can attend the sessions you want.

What are my objectives?

Write down a list of objectives for the conference. Learning, networking, creating new partnerships, looking for a new affiliate program or manager, looking for SEO help are all just a few examples of objectives.

What can I gain from attending?

You could gain new ideas, new relationships, new insights, new opportunities or more. Just envision what you want to gain, so you go with a goal in mind.

How will this conference contribute to my success?

Think of how the conference will benefit you and your business short term and long term.

When is the conference? Will it conflict with anything?

If the conference is too close to a holiday, or any commitment, it could be stressful trying to go to a conference when you're on a budget, especially if you're flying, because airfare goes up around holidays. Is the conference over the weekend? If you work for someone else, how much time will you be missing from work?

Also, don't worry about is the size of the conference. Don't assume the more people that go, the more you'll get from it. Focus more on quality, rather than quantity. Even if there happens to be some conferences that have both quality and quantity, research first.

Look for conference reviews on blogs, word of mouth on social media, and reach out to the staff and see what they are like too.

Notice in the list of questions I didn't include "How much is it?", because attending the conference is achievable if you know how to budget for it.

First, scope out the conference you are interested in, and determine if it is relevant to your blog or business. Find out what type of venue the conference will be in and the location.

Also, check to see how far the conference is from you and how much airfare will be. If the conference is in California, and you live in New York, check to see if the conference is also taking place on the east coast later in the year, or vice versa.

Section 4: Identify Your Budget

How much money you are spending each month? What are you spending it on? What is your monthly budget, and do you have one?

If you cannot answer those questions without looking at your bank account then you are probably not tracking your finances. This is why a budget is important, because you may think you can't afford something when you probably can.

In order to attend a conference, you should start putting money aside until the conference. First find out when it is. Is it in 6, 9, 12 months?

If you just hear about a conference a couple months before and you don't have it in your budget, it's better to skip that one if you can't borrow the needed money from something else in your budget.

And when it's less than a month away, the hotel group rate has likely expired, passes for the conference are often at the full price, and airfare could be increasing any day. Another thing to consider is that passes may be sold out and the hotel may be all booked up.

Now on to budgeting! First write down your short term and long term financial goals.

Next write down all your bills: rent (or mortgage) payment, utilities, insurance, car payment, groceries, business expenses, credit cards, etc.

What are you spending the most money on that is not necessary? For example it's necessary to pay bills and living expenses (rent, car payment, phone bill, etc.), but it is not necessary to eat out every night or buy coffee three times a day at a coffee shop.

How are those bar tabs adding up? Cut back on going out and drinking, because that can be one big setback for saving up money. If you really want to save money, you'll need to cut back on the little things that really add up.

Look at everything you spend and make the decision to cut back somewhere, because this will only help you work better toward your short term and long term financial goals.

When you cut back, you can start a fund for your conference expenses. For example, if I took $20 per week and saved it for a conference that is six months away, I would have approximately

$480. That would most likely cover airfare, depending on where the conference is.

What about setting aside $100 every two weeks? Can you do that? If there's a will, there's a way. If you're really gung-ho about your business, you could even cut out cable or Netflix. I don't have cable TV, and I save about $50 a month just for that, plus I am able to be more productive!

Regardless of what you do, you have to take action and cut back on something and set the extra money aside.

You pick the dollar amount that's right for you, but just try it out and you'll see just how much money you can accumulate.

Section 5: Three Tips for Staying on a Budget

Use Cash.

> Sometimes people think they spend cash quicker than they do when using a card, but it's much easier to swipe a card without thinking about it. Take out an amount that is right for you per week, and act like it's all you have. Therefore, it will be easier to control impulse buys.

Share the Responsibility.

> If you're not single, then you know that you also have to watch what your family is spending. Talk to your spouse about the budget and set up a plan together. Make this rewarding for you both, and most importantly... NO BLAMING!

> When fingers are pointed at who spends more on what, it can lead to an argument. Just take responsibility first by owning up

to what areas you know you could improve upon and say how you will change them.

If your spouse sees you owning up to your bad habits without you pointing out theirs, they may open up about their areas for improvement, too. If not, then just be the bigger person by not pointing out their faults (this advice also goes for many areas in a relationship, not just in finances).

Also, the importance of sharing the responsibility is so that there is no stress, or pressure, all on one person.

Keep Your Receipts.

Once a budget is made, sometimes people are on it for a week or two and then fall off track. By saving receipts, you can stay on track by writing down the places you went and money you spent. Once you look at it all on paper (or in an Excel spreadsheet), you may realize just how much money you're letting slip by. If you stay on track you'll be less likely to overspend.

There's also budget software called "You Need a Budget" (YNAB), if you're interested in an online system, to help you track the finances better. There is also a list of free budget templates you can Google.

Part Two:
How to Attend a Conference on a Budget

Section 1: Buying a Pass

Once you've selected the conference you want to attend, it is important to know the dates of the conference, and to check for early bird price specials. Follow the conference on social media and sign up for the mailing list to get the alerts for special/discounted pricing.

If there is a deadline date for early pricing, make sure you find out about it. You'll want to buy the pass at that early price before it goes up.

Next, you'll want to determine which pass is best for you. For example, if there is a pass for only $99, you might be excited to jump on the deal right away because it is inexpensive, but what does it include? Look to see if it only gets you in the exhibit hall and nothing else, is it worth it? Are you solely going to network or do you want to learn while you're there?

I have seen people buy the cheapest pass without looking into what it includes, only for that person to say later that they didn't read what they were getting and can only go to the exhibit hall and keynote sessions when what they really wanted was access to all sessions.

If you want to make the most of the conference and be able to go to all sessions, you might as well just get the next pass up. Look at the conference agenda and sessions ahead of time, so you can plan which sessions you want to attend. It's also worth it to do the next pass up if it includes food.

It may cost a little bit more, but it works out. If you pay a little more to have access to all parts of the conference, you're making the most of it.

Plus, think of the money you will save if food is included. That's the thing to consider, though, does it include food and what type of food?

Many conferences will include a breakfast, but some of the ones I've been to just put out bread and pastries. It's less expensive than eggs, sausages, bacon, and fruit, but it will only tide you over for a short period of time.

In fact, carbs burn the quickest. Protein and healthy fats satiate people the longest, plus the complex carbs equal sugar, and a sugar rush is only temporary, and it comes along with a crash.

Look at that... I just surprised you with some nutrition facts (I am also a nutritionist and health and wellness coach).

Anyway, the point is some conferences offer a buffet breakfast, a buffet lunch, and a snack break. If you think about the time cost and actual expense cost of going to find and buy a breakfast, snack, and lunch, it adds up.

I know in Las Vegas alone it can easily cost about $40 a meal for only one person! Don't forget the tips too. If sessions start at 9 or 10 am and you're off looking for breakfast with a few hundred, or thousand, other people the wait time is going to cost you too.

Section 2: Transportation

Depending on where you live, in relation to where the conference is taking place, may dictate on your mode of transportation. Can you take a bus, train, plane, or do a road trip by car?

If you live in California and the conference is in Las Vegas, check and compare to see the cost of a bus or plane ride. Also, if a friend or colleague is going to the conference, too, you could make a road trip out of it, and split the gas money. If the road trip would take you overnight and a hotel isn't in your budget, then forget that mode of transportation.

Look into the good old' train system. Train rides are relatively inexpensive and they're a reliable/safe way to travel. Buses may not be ideal, but a Greyhound might do the trick if you live in Massachusetts and want to get to New York without driving (it's about $40).

If you happen to live out of the country, or somewhere smack-dab in the middle of the East or West coast, and flying is the most convenient, then you will need research the best flights.

You can check the obvious sites like Priceline, Travelocity, CheapOAir, and more… but set up price alerts in advance. Also, sometimes checking the actual site can be good because the airline may host private sales.

On certain sites, you can choose the trip you want and set an alert for when prices are the cheapest. Some may only alert you even when the price only fell by $2 and that's not a whole lot. Airfarewatchdog.com can alert you when prices fall by more than just a measly $2.

Tips for Flying on Budget

- You can use the Kayak Explore tool (kayak.com/explore) to see certain destinations within a budget.

- According to a Farecompare.com smart tip, it's cheapest to book flights on a Tuesday around 3 pm.

- Also, after you book a flight, check the next morning to see if prices dropped. If they did, you can call the airline and ask to cancel and rebook without a penalty.

- Follow the airline on social media to watch for deals.

- Fly two different airlines if it's cheaper. If you find that one-way on an airline like Southwest is cheaper than the return, then check another airline for a better return flight (or vice versa).

- According to the Airlines Reporting Corporation, sometimes booking 6 weeks in advance can actually save you money because prices drop.

Section 3: Sleeping Arrangements

Hotels can be pricey, but they may also be worth it in some cases. If the conference is being held in a hotel, they usually offer special group rate prices. The best part about a group rate and staying in the conference hotel is the simple ease and convenience of staying in the same place as the event.

If the group rate is still out of your budget, try getting a room with two beds and get a roommate. If that doesn't work, then check into other hotels in the area or try Airbnb.com or even Couchsurfing.org.

If the location of the conference is on the strip in Las Vegas, I doubt Airbnb and Couchsurfing would be beneficial. Your best bet then would be to compare the conference hotel to another one nearby.

Years ago, the first time I went to a conference in Las Vegas that was at Caesar's Palace, I noticed the rate was still a little out of my budget. I checked Bally's across the street, and was able to stay there for about $300 cheaper.

I didn't mind walking across the street at all. But, I will say, now that I stay in the conference hotel at the group rate, I enjoy the ability to go to my room when I want to. Once again, sometimes the convenience is worth it!

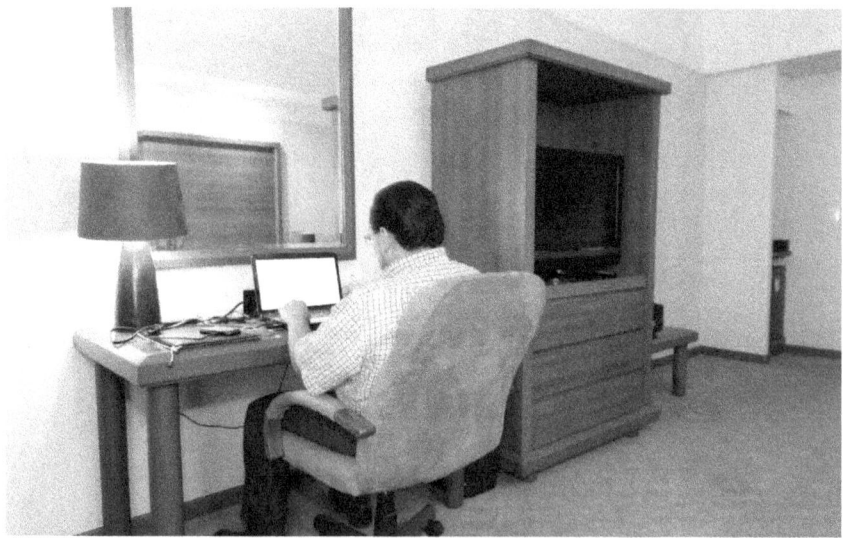

Now, let's say, for instance, the conference is somewhere in San Francisco in a decent area. Maybe then check into either Airbnb or Couchsurfing.

Also, if you don't stay at the conference hotel, look to see if there is a bus system near where you will stay and how long it will take to get to the conference. Check to see the total cost of the trips and if it's more time consuming to gauge whether it's worth it or not.

Section 4: Food/Dining Out

As I said in the section about buying a pass, the cost for the highest level pass is worth it if it involves a good food selection.

Otherwise, if your pass doesn't include food, or the conference doesn't offer what you prefer to eat, then check out places to eat in the conference area ahead of time.

If you know the location of the conference, and have the address, you can do a search on Yelp for restaurants nearby.

One big tip I want to offer, that I still do to this day due to personal food intolerances, is pack your own food (non-perishable, of course). I usually buy some different flavors of my favorite snack bars and pack about two bars a day worth for the duration of the conference.

They are small and don't take up much room, but if you don't have the room you could find a store when you get to the conference location and buy snacks.

Photo credit: Peter Fitzpatrick

I like the nutty Kind® bars, because they offer protein and omegas. Nature Valley oat bars are good and inexpensive, too. An apple and/or some oranges are good healthy choices, as well. If you have a snack during the conference, it'll do you some good between meals.

As for breakfast, lunch, and dinner… if you are not doing the conference breakfast and lunch, then look for a diner nearby, or search for places that are close and look over the menus. Check out the meals that may interest you, and the food prices ahead of time, so you can plan a budget for food.

As for beverages, carry an empty, reusable water bottle (I prefer a 32oz or larger) during the conference and refill. Water is free, it's healthy, it's easy, and it keeps you hydrated.

Some conferences may even offer complimentary beverages, so check into that, as well, if you want to get free tea or coffee.

Section 5: How to Attend a Conference for Free

There are lots of hacks to cut costs when attending a conference, but each conference will have different opportunities.

Again, I suggest following the conferences you're interested in on their social media accounts, and sign up for their newsletters for any contests that may come about, or for any other promotional opportunities.

Some conferences have a press pass opportunity, or may offer the chance at a free pass in another form. For example, Affiliate Summit offers the Pay it Forward program (a scholarship opportunity for affiliates).

Another chance to get a pass, only if you're experienced and have something to share is to look into being a speaker at the event.

Most events will provide the pass as compensation for speaking, but not airfare and hotel.

This is more of an opportunity for those in the industry a while (seasoned veterans) and not newcomers, but it never hurts to put your name out there.

Section 6: A Conference is Actually an Investment

If you think of a conference as an investment, rather than an expense, you will see it in a different way. Conferences open up opportunities and can help you learn to run your business more productively, so that you may earn more money.

Conferences can also connect you to the right people that can lead to more opportunities of financial gain.

Also, if you save your receipts, you can write off the expenses when doing your taxes (this is where tracking finances and keeping receipts come in handy).

The money you spend at a conference is an investment to your business' future and success, and I wish you the best success with your business.

www.ingramcontent.com/pod-product-compliance
Lightning Source LLC
Chambersburg PA
CBHW070728180526
45167CB00004B/1670